Let's travel in

NIGERIA

AND GHANA

By Glenn D. Kittler

Edited by Darlene Geis

A TRAVEL PRESS BOOK

SECOND PRINTING

PICTURE ACKNOWLEDGMENTS

The full-color illustrations in this book are the work of the following photographers and artists, whose collaboration is gratefully acknowledged. Photographed in Nigeria and Ghana by Stephanie Dinkins (2, 3, 4, 5, 6, 7, 9, 10, 11, 13, 14, 15, 16, 21, 22, 24, 25, 26, 27, 28, 31, 32); Harrison Forman (1, 8, 12, 17, 18, 19, 20, 23, 29, 30). For the black-and-white photographs we wish to thank Stephanie Dinkins; Harrison Forman; Brian Brake and Marc Riboud, from Magnum. The map was made by Enrico Arno.

Library of Congress Catalog Card Number: 65-28202

CONTENTS

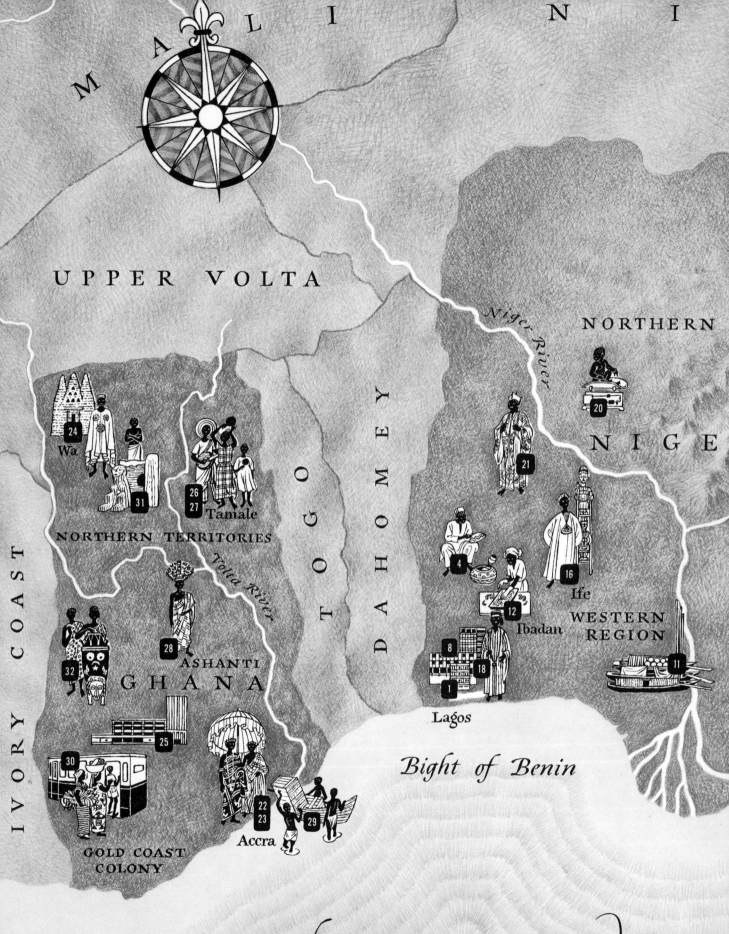

MALI

UPPER VOLTA

NIGER

NORTHERN

NIGE

Wa

24

31

26
27
Tamale

NORTHERN TERRITORIES

TOGO

DAHOMEY

Niger River

20

21

4

12

16
Ife

Ibadan

WESTERN
REGION

28

ASHANTI

GHANA

IVORY COAST

32

25

8

18

1

11

30

Lagos

22
23
Accra

29

Bight of Benin

GOLD COAST
COLONY

ATLANTIC OCEAN

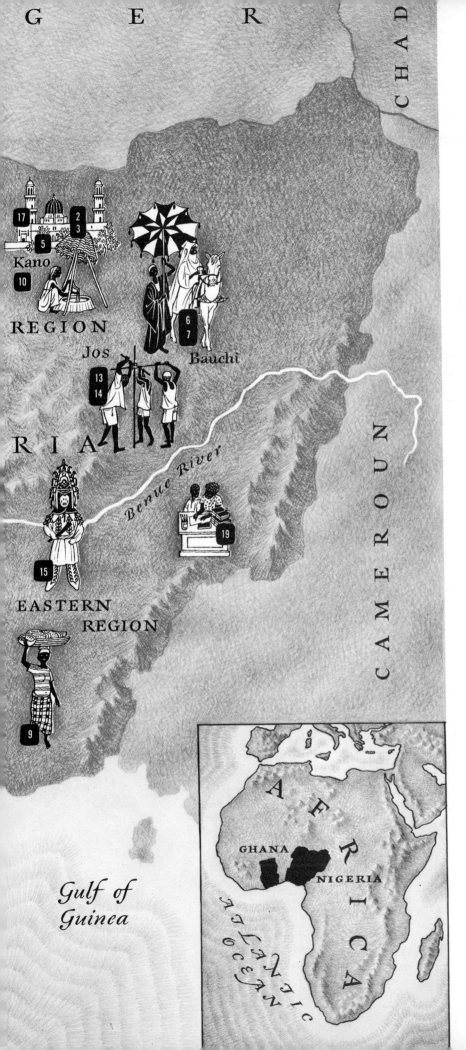

Locales of thirty-two full-page pictures

NIGERIA AND GHANA:

NEW LANDS OF FREEDOM

WHAT fascinating countries they are, these two new independent nations in Africa's western bulge. The future hopes of all Africa rest with them. Nigeria (*nigh*-JEER-*ih-uh*) and Ghana (GAH-*nuh*) are to today's world what the thirteen American colonies were to the world of yesterday: their conduct in their new freedom will affect democracies for centuries to come. If, as many hope, there will one day be an all-African federation, the pattern for it is being set now in these two young nations.

What are they like? How does their land look? Who are their people? To answer these questions we must go on a voyage of discovery to these two new countries that are making such challenging claims to world attention. Nigeria's thirty-eight million inhabitants make it most populous nation on the African continent, the twelfth in the world. Ghana, the former Gold Coast Colony, was the first new African nation in one hundred years and the first Negro member of the British Commonwealth.

Situated almost midway between the Mediterranean and the Cape of Good Hope, Nigeria and Ghana comprise a distinct hub of the new Africa. To the north is the vast and mysterious Moslem world of the Sahara, as steeped in Mohammedan traditions as Mecca itself; to the south is the throbbing subcontinent of Black Africa, where tribal chiefs and witch doctors are still men of great power. Both cultures have deeply influenced Nigeria and Ghana in the past; now Nigeria and Ghana share the daring opportunity of influencing both cultures in the future.

THE DARK PAST

Africa was a forgotten part of the world for centuries. At one time the African city-state of Carthage grew so powerful that its general Hannibal almost conquered Rome. But the Moslem sweep across North Africa in 661 severed the continent from Europe, lowering a Sand Curtain which not even the Crusades could effectively penetrate. Moslem

In northern Nigeria a horseman wears flowing Arab robes and chain mail believed to be a relic from the Crusades.

pirates roamed the Mediterranean and the Atlantic, terrorizing European merchant ships that ventured from their ports. Eight hundred years later, the unification of Spain provided the military power to push the invading Moors southward, beyond Gibraltar, thus freeing the oceans for such great seamen as Vasco da Gama and Christopher Columbus. With that began the first important European probings of the West African coast.

Meanwhile, the areas that became Nigeria and Ghana were already feeling the influence of foreigners who arrived by land. The most significant of these were the Arab merchants who struggled across the dangerous Sahara in search of markets. The Arabic approach was slow but steady, gradual but enduring. By the thirteenth century, Moslem influence had spread to the northern regions of Nigeria and Ghana, there to remain an important factor even to this day.

EMPIRE BUILDERS

When the European explorers first reached West Africa, they approached it from the coast, in areas free from Moslem influence. Just as Arab merchants had crossed the desert to trade salt for grain, leather and indigo dyes, so the Europeans sailed down the coast of Africa to barter cloth, trinkets and weapons for ivory, pepper and gold. When they began to penetrate the interior in search of new trading posts, however, the Europeans found the same religious obstacles that were blocking them along the Mediterranean, for Moslemism required that its followers associate only with their own kind. Inland trade became for the Europeans not barter but conquest. Only one African commodity was so valuable to both groups that there were no barriers to its traffic—slaves.

In the two hundred and fifty years of Africa's booming slave trade, over twenty million people were captured and carried away from the Nigeria-Ghana region alone, leaving the area permanently scarred socially, economically and emotionally. The people now had a bitter memory that would be a long time in fading, and no matter what good the Europeans might later try to do for Africa this scar would always remain. All European countries that engaged in the exploration of Africa likewise engaged in slave traffic. Also, the national boundaries that were subsequently set up in Africa were determined by Europeans, regardless of the history, culture or ethnic groups of the natives. It was no wonder, then, that there was seldom peace, that there were frequent tribal flare-ups against one another and against the foreign authority.

From about 1800, the authority in the Nigeria and Ghana areas was England. In 1807, the British Parliament abolished slavery throughout the empire, but some fifty years passed before the law was effectively enforced in the zones of British interest along the Gulf of Guinea (GHIN-*ih*). From the coastal settlement trading interests moved deeper and deeper inland during the last half of the nineteenth century, and with the support of British troops the trading rights expanded into colonial rights. By the turn of the century both Nigeria and Ghana were officially, as they had long been actually, colonies of the Crown.

NIGERIA—LAND AND PEOPLE

Some scientists believe the human race came into being in Africa instead of Asia, as is generally held, and at Ife (EE-*feh*), in Nigeria's Western Region, is a statue grove which the Yoruba (YOR-*oo-bah*) tribesmen will tell you marks the site of man's first home. In 1485, when the Portuguese arrived at Benin (*beh*-NIN), on the Niger (NIGH-*jer*) River delta, they found the people producing bronze statuary of great delicacy, finer than any bronze work being created by the artists of Europe. But the absence of written records from that period is evidence of Nigeria's severe isolation from the rest of the developing world.

Isolated Nigeria had long been a haven for roaming African tribes who sought to escape the dangers—enemies, disease, famine—in their homelands. Today there are over two hundred and fifty tribes in Nigeria and there are twelve distinct languages, some of them highly complex. The greatest tribes became empires ruled by mighty kings, with elaborate palaces and mosques, magnificent costumes and highly developed arts and crafts.

Language, religion, tradition and alliances caused Nigeria to develop into three regions—Northern, Western, Eastern. The Niger River with its tributary, the Benue (BAY-*nway*), forms a Y-shaped division of the country that coincides with the three regions. The Northern Region,

11

above the Niger and Benue, is the largest—about the size of France. The Western and Eastern Regions are divided by the lower Niger, and its branches form their northern boundaries.

Each region is uniquely different, both in culture and in nature. The Moslem Northern Region is semidesert, but contains most of the country's valuable ores. The rest of Nigeria is, like most of Africa, richly verdant and produces the country's agricultural exports. The Yorubas in the Western Region already had a well-organized government by the time the British took power, while the Ibos (EE-*boze*) in the Eastern Region were retarded by a primitive clan system which they retained until recent years.

The British developed their colony on the regional basis. As early as 1914, two men from each region served as advisors to the British governor-general. Over the years, Nigerians took an increasing role in their government, and in 1954 a federation of regions was created with an eye to national independence. On October 1, 1960, independence was proclaimed. Thus Nigeria smoothly assumed its role in the British Commonwealth as a new and free nation.

GHANA: GOLD AND CHOCOLATE

A thousand years ago there existed in western Africa a mighty nation called Ghana, and so when the Gold Coast received its independence on March 6, 1957, it changed its name to Ghana as an indication of its hopes for itself. Since then, Ghana has proved to be a sprightly country, impatient to become involved in world affairs, and perhaps this youthful exuberance is a sign of its future role.

Ghana's road to independence was not as smooth as Nigeria's. For years there was political agitation, and only after each uprising did the people acquire greater influence in the government. Sadly, the riots of 1948 took many lives, but out of them came British concessions that led first to the Ghanaians' control of their internal affairs in 1952, and eventually to full independence within the Commonwealth.

Like Nigeria, Ghana developed into three regions—the populous Gold Coast Colony at the south, the powerful Kingdom of the Ashantis (*uh*-SHAN-*tihz*) in the central province, and the arid, neglected flatlands of the Northern Territories—and they were as distinctly different and divided as their Nigerian counterparts. Kwame Nkrumah (KVAH-*meh n'*KROO-*mah*), who led the final freedom riots and became the country's first president, had hoped for a centralized form of government, but he failed to reckon with Ashanti chiefs who were fearful of losing their local powers. The result was a federation under a national government that could be only as strong as its popularity allowed. Nkrumah was popular, but he faced an active opposition that at times drove him to unwise extremes, such as press censorship and the exile of critics. Among the young, however, Nkrumah was still the hero who gave them their freedom.

It was gold that first made Ghana attractive, slavery that made it important, but cocoa that made it rich. Today, gold remains a major export; slavery, of course, is gone; and cocoa is the basis of Ghana's economy. Ghana produces one-third of the world's cocoa supply, about half of it purchased by the United States. Cocoa enables Ghana to be one of the few African countries that exports more than it imports, a healthy factor. And yet one bad crop could make the government inoperable; two consecutive bad crops would mean national bankruptcy.

Modern civilization has come to Africa— though it sometimes arrives by primitive methods.

Early in his career, Nkrumah was warned that insects attacking the cocoa trees would eventually ruin the nation's extensive cocoa forests unless drastic measures were taken. The infected trees had to be destroyed and, as a preventive measure, a surrounding belt of healthy trees had to be sacrificed in order to prevent further spread of the blight. Ordering such action would deprive thousands of small farmers of their lone money crop, a stunning blow that could mean political suicide to the man who ordered it. Taking the long view, Nkrumah gave the order, and after a few years the bewildered, anguished farmers discovered that he had been right. The cocoa forests were saved, and a courageous government proved itself to be more effective than one that merely made a bid for popular approval.

HEADLONG PLUNGE INTO THE FUTURE

Effective national courage, however, requires mutual trust between the people and their governments. As yet, this trust has not significantly appeared in either Nigeria or Ghana. Old suspicions and feuds rooted in tribalism and religious differences have kept the two countries seriously divided internally.

And thus, instead of presenting themselves to the watching world as unified nations, strong in their new independence, Ghana and Nigeria have shown an unfortunate weakness. They have subdivided their

13

regions into small domains to satisfy each minority group. This danger-ous tendency exists throughout Africa, which has yet to grasp the demo-cratic ideal that subordinates minority interests to the common good while guaranteeing each group full opportunity and freedom.

Fortunately, young Nigerians and Ghanaians who have had the ad-vantages of studying here and in Europe have brought new concepts home with them. We see the results of what they have learned in their recent efforts to provide a better way of life for all in their homelands. We see better schools, improved health services, broader opportunities spreading throughout their lands. In such efforts lies the hope of these two new nations, and it is this hope that makes their future so exciting.

British law and justice have had a profound influence on Nigeria and Ghana.

let's travel in

NIGERIA

AND GHANA

MODERN LAGOS: AFRICAN METROPOLIS

YOUR first impression of Nigeria depends upon where you enter the country. Arriving at Lagos (LAH-*gohs*), the capital city, you find yourself surrounded by modern skyscrapers, bustling traffic, good shops and fine hotels. You wonder: Can this be Africa?

Yes, this is indeed Africa, the new Africa, rushing forward to its new place in the world with the speed of the jet that brought you here. You feel this in Lagos more than anywhere else in Africa. A few years ago, the city was merely Nigeria's major port, functioning in quiet British efficiency. But then, as independence neared, Lagos was made a federal district, center of the government, and the building boom was on. Suddenly Lagos was a world capital, cosmopolitan, vital, aware of its new importance.

Should you, on the other hand, decide to enter Nigeria from Kano in the Northern Region an entirely different world awaits you. Kano is one of the oldest cities of North Africa, and it was a thriving market place

On the edge of the Sahara, the ancient city of Kano links central Africa to the Arab world.

for desert caravans a thousand years ago, when Lagos was only a cluster of grass huts. Kano today with its maze of mud huts is home to almost a hundred thousand people, whose customs are old as their city. Here you have them—two cities, two worlds—each contributing the best of themselves to the future of the young country.

16

KANO AIRPORT: HERALDING THE FUTURE

EVEN in ancient Kano the startling contrasts of Nigeria are dramatically apparent, for Kano has a new air terminal, one of the finest in the world. Standing proudly on the threshold of the Sahara, the beautiful building towers over a long, sleek runway—and down the runway comes a shepherd leading his small flock. Why not? It is easier to get home this way than over the fields.

And here another contrast exists: the herald with his seven-foot trumpet. Dozens of times each day he blasts the warning: "Danger! Everybody off the runway! A plane is coming!" He has a different tune for take-offs. The trumpet, called a *kakaki* (kah-kah-KEE), is made in three sections, and when not in use it is taken apart and carried in a leather bag. A royal musical instrument, the *kakaki* is traditionally played in public only on special occasions—which Kano's new jet traffic surely is.

Today, Nigeria has its government-owned airline, Nigeria Airways, whose skillful pilots are the sons of bushmen who probably never even rode in a car. And so another contrast, from generation to generation. The passengers are a diverse lot. Here is a young man returning to his studies at Oxford or Yale. The veiled woman sitting alone in the corner is on her way to visit her parents in Tripoli. Near the door is a group of government officials, en route to an important session of the United Nations. And stepping off the jet that just arrived is a Moslem chief who has made his visit to Mecca, the holy city in Saudi Arabia. For centuries the journey to Mecca was so long, arduous and expensive that those who made it were assured their places in Paradise. Now the four-thousand-mile round trip can be made over a weekend. Thus progress has brought a unique advantage to Nigerian Moslems. It is easier now to get into heaven.

18

INDIGO DYE PITS: GOAL OF THE CARAVANS

THERE is no blue like Nigerian blue. This was common knowledge centuries ago, when desert caravans were bringing bolts of cloth from the Mediterranean shores to be dyed in the Kano indigo pits. Why blue? It is beautiful—and it cuts down the glare of the desert sun.

Made from the fermented leaves of the indigo plant, which grows wild in the area, the dye is poured into ten-foot-deep pits in the Kano market place. All day, workers dip cloth into the dye until it acquires the desired hue. After the cloth dries, it is taken into a nearby hut where men spread it on a log and beat it with heavy wooden mallets coated with butter and glue. Gradually the cloth takes on the gorgeous sheen that so distinctly marks it a Kano product.

This is the oldest industry of Nigeria, and its process has remained unchanged for more than a thousand years. Scientists have devised techniques for duplicating indigo dye in laboratories, but the Kano workers would not think of using it. Why change what is already good? It is an African philosophy that often retards progress. In Kano department stores, you can buy canned foods from London, Chicago and Johannesburg, but in the market place merchants spread their local wares on the ground, while strolling players beat their drums for the small coins in your pocket. This was good enough for your father; isn't it good enough for you?

A Nigerian market is lively with the sound of drums played by strolling musicians.

21

CALABASH CARVERS: HEIRS OF AN OLD TRADITION

THE Yoruba tribesmen's talent for arts and crafts turns sometimes to humble materials. In the market place of Oyo (oh-*yoh*) we see the calabash carvers who make decorative objects out of what is actually a vegetable. The calabash is a pumpkin-like plant that has been cultivated by the North Africans from earliest times. When the pulp is removed, the hollow gourd can be used as a container for food or water, or even made into a musical instrument.

Nigeria has a great artistic tradition that goes back to the remarkable portrait heads sculptured by the Yoruba people as early as the sixth century. Although their modern art is not up to the standards of the past, the Yoruba still have a fine sense of design and a love of decoration. An ordinary calabash gourd is beautified by their skillful workmanship.

Balancing a tray of home-baked loaves on her head, this bread vendor helps balance the family budget, too.

A man must work a whole day to carve and decorate one of the large containers, which he can then sell for about fifty-six cents. That is scarcely enough to support his family, so his wife helps by trading in the nearby market place. The Yoruba calabash carver, like artists all over the world, alas, needs the help and support of a sympathetic wife.

MOSLEM MANSION: FORTRESS OF PRIVACY

A RICH man lives in this beautiful house in the Northern Region, and its almost windowless façade lets the world know that its owner cherishes his privacy. But the poor man, living in a mud house down the street, wants the same privacy, and his walls, too, shut the world out. And yet—Allah has ordered it—no hungry stranger is turned away from a Moslem home. He is fed and he may stay the night if he wishes, in a special guest room near the front door, but he is not allowed into the interior.

The basic reason for such guarded seclusion is women. Once a woman enters her husband's house, she seldom leaves it, and then only when she is heavily veiled. The Moslem religion allows a man to have four wives, but he can have as many concubines as he can afford. The first wife is like a mother to the others and she runs the household. She must also approve of any other women who follow her into the family circle. In a house as grand as this, there are undoubtedly many servants, so the women have little to do. Deep in the interior is a courtyard where they spend most of their day, singing and playing a musical instrument called the *shantu* (*shahn*-TOO), which is played only in harems and is not supposed to be heard by men.

During her first year of marriage, a Moslem bride must complain about how badly her husband treats her and how she longs to return to her parents. She does so in song, tapping out accompaniment on a *shantu*. But she does not really mean it; she is merely extending a traditional courtesy to her parents. It would be considered an insult to her family if she could be happy when so recently separated from them. Actually, if she has been lucky enough to marry into a rich household like this, she knows she is better off than she ever was.

25

FESTIVAL:
ALL HAIL
THE EMIR

THE gates swing open; out rides the Emir of Bauchi (BOUGH-*chee*); a great cheer rises from the crowd. This is Salah (SAH-*lah*), the great Moslem feast, and the Emir will lead the celebrations. His turbaned bodyguard is at his side; his umbrella bearer protects him from the sun. Before him, the chiefs who serve under him are waiting to pay their homage.

Bauchi is in the eastern part of the Northern Region, a Moslem stronghold, and thus Salah—the day of Allah—is fervently observed. Moslems in Mecca on this day are especially blessed, but few of the world's four hundred million Moslems can be there, so the feast is celebrated from Morocco to Indonesia by the faithful. Here in Bauchi, there are solemn religious ceremonies and gay festivities.

The Emir is an important man. In 1903, the British created seven emirates in the Northern Region, each with its ruling feudal lord, and this handsome young man on the magnificent stallion is the descendant of one of them. Independence has diminished his authority considerably; he can no longer levy taxes for his own use nor is he any longer the ultimate law of his district. Nevertheless, he is still greatly admired and respected, and his people are delighted to see him on one of his rare public appearances.

Now the Emir will go to an open field beyond the palace where he will take a position at one end. At the opposite end his chiefs gather, as many as fifty of them, mounted on spirited horses. Two by two they come charging up to the Emir at full gallop; they rein in their horses at the last moment and salute him, shouting his praises and pledging their loyalty. Then they wheel around and gallop off, to be followed by another pair of chiefs. Afterwards, the Emir will take his place in the grandstands and the chiefs will race on their finest horses. The prizes: gifts from the Emir himself.

26

ROYAL
DRUMMER:
MAKE WAY!
MAKE WAY!

NOW the Emir's retinue begins its return to the palace. Just behind the Emir comes the royal drummer, a celebrity himself. His drums are called *tamboura* (*tam-boo*-RAH), and their use is governed by rigid protocol. Only the drummer of a great emir is permitted to play them, and their public use is limited to occasions when an emir is enthroned, when he takes to the field of battle and at Moslem festivals.

Tamboura are played in pairs, one tenor and one bass. In processions, they are always carried on camelback with the drummer seated cross-legged behind them. But for the emir's private pleasure the drums are played in his palace each Thursday evening—the eve of the Moslem sabbath. Most of the Islamic pageantry takes place in the north of Nigeria. Moslems comprise forty-four per cent of the national population, but in the Northern Region the Islamic majority is twice that. In the south, the tribal music and dancing stem from a different background, completely unlike the formalized Moslem tradition. Small wonder the two groups find it difficult to see eye to eye.

Tribesmen, coated with oil and arrayed in harvest symbols, dance to celebrate a good crop.

GOVERNMENT
RADIO:
DISC JOCKEY

A NEW sound is heard in the land—radio, complete with commercials. As in England, broadcasting facilities are government-owned but operated by corporations. In Nigeria, however, each region has its own radio corporation apart from the Nigerian Broadcasting Corporation in Lagos. In its first year—1961—the federal station earned fifteen thousand dollars from commercials, and was considered highly successful. The Western Region, the country's most progressive area, has television, but the sets cost almost a hundred and fifty dollars, a fortune in Nigerian terms, and so there is only a small audience.

Language is the major broadcasting difficulty. The Lagos radio broadcasts in English and fifteen other languages and dialects. The native languages differ so greatly that an announcement may take ten minutes in one language and only three in another. As a result of this Tower of Babel broadcasting, the average Nigerian listener doesn't understand a

These energetic performers are hot musicians in every sense of the word.

word of what is coming over his radio a good deal of the time. Thus music constitutes most of the Nigerian programming. The heavier the beat, the more rhythmic the melody, the better Nigerians like it, which accounts for the popularity of American jazz and rock-and-roll. When the disc jockey spins a platter, his audience enjoys it in any language.

FOREST PATH:
WOMEN CARRY
THE BURDENS

THEIR morning's shopping at the village market completed, three women wend their way home through the palm forests of the Eastern Region. As always, they carry their burdens on their heads. Actually, this is far less tiring than carrying packages in their arms and less troublesome than handbags. Besides, African women are naturally graceful, and once their packages are properly balanced on their heads they can walk along with the ease and confidence of a fashion model. Men, too, carry things on their heads, but toting is rightly a woman's job and no man would think of doing it as long as his wife was available.

The palm trees of the Eastern Region are an important source of income to the people. Palm nuts produce an edible oil, rich in vitamin A, which Nigerians pour on baked yams, boiled bananas and into stews. It is also used as medicine and in juju—African magic—rituals. But that is not all. This versatile product is inflammable and serves as lamp fuel, too. Commercially, the oil is much in demand in America and elsewhere for the manufacture of soap, and the first palm nuts were exported to England at the time of the Spanish Armada.

Producing palm oil is a family business, but so are almost all activities in the Eastern Region. Unlike the people in the rest of the country, Easterners have never submitted themselves to the rule of powerful paramount chiefs or emirs but have kept their society at a more primitive clan level. Clans have divided up the palm forests along the coastal regions and nobody would dare cross the line from one family's grove to another. Whole families are engaged in gathering the red fruit, steaming it in earthenware pots, then pounding the fleshy part into a pulp. When this is mixed with cold water, the oil floats to the top and is scooped off. Recently the government, in hopes of increasing production, has tried to introduce a plantation system with modern equipment, but tradition runs deep in Africa and the clans will not surrender their historic rights in the forests.

MARKET IN
KANO:
MECCA FOR
TRAVELERS

WOULD you like to try a kola nut? Here in the Kano market they are a fast-moving item. Deep trays of reddish nuts are on sale every few feet and you buy the nuts by the cupful. Nigerians, especially in the north, eat them like popcorn, spitting out the pulp when the juice is gone. The only trouble with kola nuts is that you might become addicted. They are bitter and juicy, rich in caffein and contain a bit of strychnine, and although they will give you something of a lift you may find them habit-forming. Kola nuts have another disadvantage: they discolor your teeth. Maybe you'd better leave them alone.

Peanuts then? Called groundnuts here, they too are found in abundance. A mainstay of the Northern diet, they are also an important export. Throughout the countryside you can see towering pyramids of green nuts, stored in the open while awaiting shipment to all parts of the world.

The Kano market is a fascinating place. On a good day, fifty thousand people from all parts of Africa flock here, seeking everything from airplane parts to witchcraft supplies. There is never a dull moment. When you are not haggling over prices with merchants, you can watch snake charmers and magicians or listen to street bands and troubadours. Keep in mind that the shows are not free: the performers expect a tip. They call it "dash" and will scream the word at you if you walk away without giving them anything.

You hear many south Nigerian dialects in the market place, for more than twenty thousand Southerners have moved into the Northern Region to take jobs that require special skills and literacy. Because of fatalistic Moslemism, which does not encourage self-improvement, the educational facilities in the north have developed slowly. But that is changing now that independence has shown the need for trained people in all fields.

NIGER HOUSEBOATS: FLOATING SUPERMARKET

EVEN here in the heart of Nigeria, people have learned the advantage of buying wholesale. Merchants in the cluster of riverboats at the steps of the Onitsha (*oh*-NICH-*ah*) market in Eastern Province undersell their competitors who rent stalls in the town's huge market place. Onitsha has always had an enormous market attracting many farmers who sold their produce there. For their convenience, the market was modernized in 1957 at the cost of a million dollars. The market's thatch-roofed stalls were replaced by three thousand tin-roofed stalls, and steps and sidewalks were constructed to make it easier for the farmers to carry their produce from their boats to the stalls. However, the steps also made it easier for shoppers to get down to the waterfront. It didn't take long for the low-overhead, no-middleman approach to attract customers to the Niger riverboats.

The Niger is among the wonders of Africa. Centuries ago, explorers thought it was the western end of the Nile: surely there could not be two such mighty rivers in one continent. Twenty-six hundred miles long, the Niger is longer than the Volga and its delta is broader than the Nile's. It rises far away in Guinea, sweeps northward in a gigantic arc, then southward through Nigeria to the sea. Because of the country's inadequate road system, the river is still the main artery of travel into the interior.

The rivers of Nigeria are important highways, carrying people and cargo deep within the land.

37

IBADAN CANNERY: BETTER FOOD, BETTER LIVES

BECAUSE most of Nigeria lacks electrical power, the problem of preserving perishable foods without refrigeration is serious. An important step toward solving it has been the opening of the Lafia (LAH-*fee-yah*) canning factory at Ibadan (*ee*-BAH-*dahn*) in the Western Region. Now Nigeria cans grapefruit, pineapple, meats and vegetables in quantities that not only assure a balanced diet to the people but also allow for export.

Sadly, improper diet is a health danger throughout Africa, growing out of several factors. African farms are small, and farmers must use every inch to grow as much of their cash crop as they can. The family eats mostly what it grows, and if there is any variety in the menu it is available only when there is money for it—when the crop is sold at harvest time. So you see African children with distended bellies indicating malnutrition, and adults suffering from the lethargy that is caused

The future may be unknown, but at least it is brighter for this generation of African youths than ever before.

by vitamin deficiency. Weak and ill, the people cannot work; unable to work, they cannot produce the food they need; lacking proper food, they remain weak and ill. That is changing now in Nigeria. The fresh fruit surplus along the coast is being canned and shipped to the less fortunate north. The Fulani (*foo*-LAH-*nee*) cattle of the north are butchered, canned and shipped to the south. Nigeria is eating better, thus living better, and facing its future with greater strength.

THE JOS PLATEAU: PROSPECTING FOR TIN

BLACK sand," the people called it; but when news of the dark soil reached Lagos at the turn of the century, engineers were sure that the black powder was tin. And it could not have been in a more inaccessible place. The Jos (JAWSS) Plateau in the center of the Northern Region rose like an island three thousand feet above the surrounding countryside, and upon its broad semidesert plains lived tribes of primitive head-hunters.

The prize was worth the risk. In 1903, when the first engineers climbed the escarpment, a chief sent word that he would have them killed if they did not leave immediately. Daringly, the engineers camped just outside the village walls for two days before they casually packed and departed. The chief sent a message: "You left just in time. But you can come back now." With that, Nigeria's tin industry was born.

The arid soil of the plateau is so loose that simple prospecting drills of the kind shown here can be used, thus eliminating expensive modern equipment. Work teams operate the hand drill by rotating the rods over their heads, co-ordinating their efforts by syncopated grunts. The drill can go down sixty feet, but that is seldom necessary on the mineral-rich plateau.

For years a side product of Nigerian tin was being discarded, but then it was identified as columbite, a metallic element essential in the manufacture of the best heat-resisting steel used in jet engines. Today, Nigeria produces three-fourths of the world's columbite, and the aircraft industry buys a large share of it. If it weren't for Nigerian columbite, modern jets wouldn't be as excellent as they are.

NIGERIAN LABORERS: OPEN-AIR MINING

MOST of Nigeria's tin ore is so close to the surface that a heavy rain can wash away the topsoil and expose it. These workers, digging and washing the ore by hand, are actually doing all that has to be done to mine the tin. When they finish in this area, the sluices clearing the topsoil for them will be channeled in a new direction and they will start all over.

All mining on the plateau was done in this way until railroad service was extended to Jos shortly before World War I. It was then possible to bring in heavy equipment to remove the topsoil in places where the tin veins were too deep to reach by the usual methods. The huge earth-moving machines, with booms two hundred feet long, can build a mountain in a day.

But tin is not the only treasure hidden in Nigeria's ground. Recently, coal was discovered near Enugu (*eh*-NOO-*goo*), capital of the Eastern Region, and the mines produce almost a million tons a year. Farther south along the coast, prospectors struck oil, bringing in more than a million tons a year. Deposits of lead, zinc and iron ore have been located as well, but in such remote areas that the power and transportation to exploit them have still to be installed. Quite definitely, the future financial security of Nigerians is right there in the good earth under their feet.

The tin industry uses powerful machinery— but it also uses women with baskets on their heads.

SECOND FUNERAL: A JOYOUS OCCASION

IN EASTERN Nigeria important men get two funerals, a tribal custom that has a sordid history. Formerly, the chiefs of the Ibos, the principal tribe of the region, did not enjoy going to their eternal rewards alone and often their wives and slaves were killed in order to accompany them. Understandably, wives and slaves took off for the woods when a chief died. A way had to be found to prevent them from doing so.

This was arranged by keeping the chief's death a secret until his unfortunate entourage had been properly sent off to join him. Then the death was announced and the tribe gathered to mourn him with feasting and dancing. The climax of the wake was the appearance of the witch doctor wearing a hideous mask and armed with a machete. Representing the evil spirits, he danced among the mourners, punishing the enemies of the chief. This usually broke up the party in a hurry.

Today the custom has, happily, been considerably modified. Men of importance—by wealth, status or accomplishments—are still buried promptly and surreptitiously, but they are not provided with companions. Usually most people know the man has died, but they keep a respectful silence until the family is ready for the public announcement at the second funeral. Because of the expense of providing food and drink for all, months may pass before the family can afford the festivities, even years if the dead man was a chief. Until the second funeral, however, the deceased man's estate is not distributed among his heirs but is held in trust.

Christianity has eliminated many of the witch doctors, and now a tribal dancer represents the evil spirits, making this part of the ceremony much safer. Even so, the dancers occasionally are carried away by their role and a few people get nicked. For this reason, wooden machetes are growing increasingly popular.

ROYALTY
AT IFE:
A PARAMOUNT
CHIEF

DIGNIFIED and stern, a paramount chief stands at the doorway of the royal reception hall at Ife in the Western Region. He is the deputy of the Oni (OH-*nee*), or ruler, of the area and the beaded pendant he wears indicates that he is also an important member of a secret cult. Ife is the spiritual capital of the Yoruba tribe, where their most sacred relics are kept.

Most Yorubas are pagans. Thus at the entrance to this pavilion where court cases are heard, figurines of Yoruba gods stand to remind the people to be honest and fair. Swearing on the Bible would naturally mean nothing to the Yorubas. Their principal deity is the god of iron and he is represented by a heavy chain that lies in a circle on the floor in front of the judges. Witnesses must stand within the circle of iron when they swear to tell the truth in this courtroom.

Standing before a shrine of the Yoruba god of thunder, these wooden statues are specimens of an ancient skill.

Though they are pagans, the Yorubas are not primitive. Theirs was a flourishing kingdom as early as the thirteenth century and the magnificent bronzes found here and at Benin are the remains of Nigeria's highest culture. Because of the Yorubas, the Western Region is the most progressive area in Nigeria today, boasting an excellent university, fine hospitals, thriving industry and a forward-looking government.

46

MOSQUE AT KANO: A TIME TO PRAY

RISING above the low mud and plaster houses of Kano is this domed mosque with its tall minarets. Five times a day the muezzin (*moo*-ehz-*in*) stands on the balcony of the minaret and cries out the call to prayer. Hundreds of faithful Moslems respond by forming lines in the surrounding fields. They are facing east toward Mecca, birthplace of Mohammed, who founded their religion. On a word from the muezzin, they will all kneel and put their foreheads to the ground. In unison they will pray aloud, asking Allah to bless and protect them.

Nearly half of Nigeria's people are Moslems, following the religion brought to them by the Arabs many centuries ago. Moslem tolerance of polygamy, which coincides with pagan tribal practices, is probably one reason that Islam won so many African converts. It is essentially a man's religion and women play scarcely any part in it. A significant fact is that only in Nigeria's heavily Islamic Northern Region have women been denied the right to vote. Kano and the other cities of the north seem the least touched, in many respects, by the changing centuries. Yet independence is having its effect here at last. Factories and schools are being built in the north, too, and they will inevitably alter the static world of the orthodox Moslem emirs.

The gateway of an emir's palace is a striking example of Moslem design.

LAGOS
CHURCH:
THEY COME
OUT SINGING

IN LAGOS, religion has a different atmosphere, for here Christianity has attracted many converts. There seems to be more vitality in the air, more determination to move ahead. Women are more in evidence in church affairs, like these who join their husbands in a hymn at the end of a Sunday service.

There are over seven million Christians in Nigeria, most of them living in the southern area, but even in the pagan Yoruba cities and the Moslem strongholds of the north you will come upon the attractive white churches with the cross rising from their steeples.

Unquestionably, Christian missionaries contributed heavily to the development which led Nigeria to independence. The Christian precepts of equality and brotherhood first alerted the Nigerians to their rights as human beings. The country's first schools were thatch-roofed structures, with just one wall to keep out the rain, built by missionaries. During the colonial administration education was entrusted to missionaries, supported by government funds. The same was true of hospitals.

This handsome white church in Lagos is one of the many new buildings that grace the capital.

And the missionaries are still at work. In the back country, they remain the most penetrating influence for freedom. Among the people still gripped by fierce chiefs and terrifying witch doctors, the missionaries preach: "God gave men minds to think for themselves."

50

HOPE OF THE
LAND:
EDUCATION

NIGERIA has a new rallying cry: "Give us education!" When America asked what type of Peace Corps personnel Nigeria could use, the quick response was: "Send us teachers!" From one end of the country to the other, the quest for knowledge is intense and insatiable.

Ten years ago, Nigeria had less than half a million students in its schools; today there are more than two and a half million in primary schools alone. Also, Nigeria now has more of its young adults studying in British and American universities than any other African country. Most of them are receiving government aid, a sign that their nation considers their education an investment in the country's future, rather than a mere advantage for the individual.

This hunger for learning is understandable. While it was a colony, there was small chance in Nigeria for anyone to rise particularly high in government or the professions; high positions were filled by Englishmen. Self-government changed that. Now the people must look to themselves for leadership of all kinds. Since positive, effective leadership can come only from an educated people, the new Nigeria put heavy emphasis on schools, more schools, better schools.

When the new Nigerian administration prepared its first annual budget, it apportioned a higher percentage for education than most of the countries of the world. Construction was planned for two new universities, hundreds of high schools, thousands of primary schools, trade schools and agriculture schools.

Thus it is now possible for youngsters like the intent lad shown here to begin the great adventure of learning at teacher's elbow and to know that, eagerly awaiting them years later, there will be professors in college lecture halls. In assuring its young people of this future, the country insures its own progress.

INFANT CARE:
ANOTHER
OUNCE,
ANOTHER TEAR

WHAT an indignity! The naked baby sits upon the scales and howls—and nobody pays attention. Well, people have other things to think about. The question: has the handsome, husky brute lost an ounce or gained one? Chances are, now that the government has instituted a nation-wide pediatrics program, he has gained his ounce—and more. No doubt about it, his lungs are in good shape.

There is also no doubt that Nigeria's new child-care program is one of the most commendable projects of the young country. In the past Nigeria, like most of Africa, suffered a high infant mortality rate. Mothers lacked proper care and training, children were born in mud huts and even at roadsides, and from the moment of birth the babies fought a losing battle against malnutrition and disease.

Today, mother and child can obtain free medical attention starting a month before birth and continuing until three months after it. To be sure, the service is available more readily in cities and large towns, where the finest equipment can be centrally located for the advantage of the greatest number. But each month the program is extended deeper into the bush, where infant mortality is highest, and the day is near when no mother need fear for the life of her baby.

Nigeria is trying to hasten that day by producing its own doctors. Until recently, Nigerians entering medicine had to go abroad for their studies. Now the University Medical College at Ibadan is graduating fifty doctors a year; by 1975, the country's four universities will be producing four hundred doctors a year. But no matter how many doctors Nigeria has, they will always be outnumbered by yowling babies who sit on scales and wonder why somebody doesn't pay attention to them instead of to charts. And yet it is because of the charts that there will be more healthy babies.

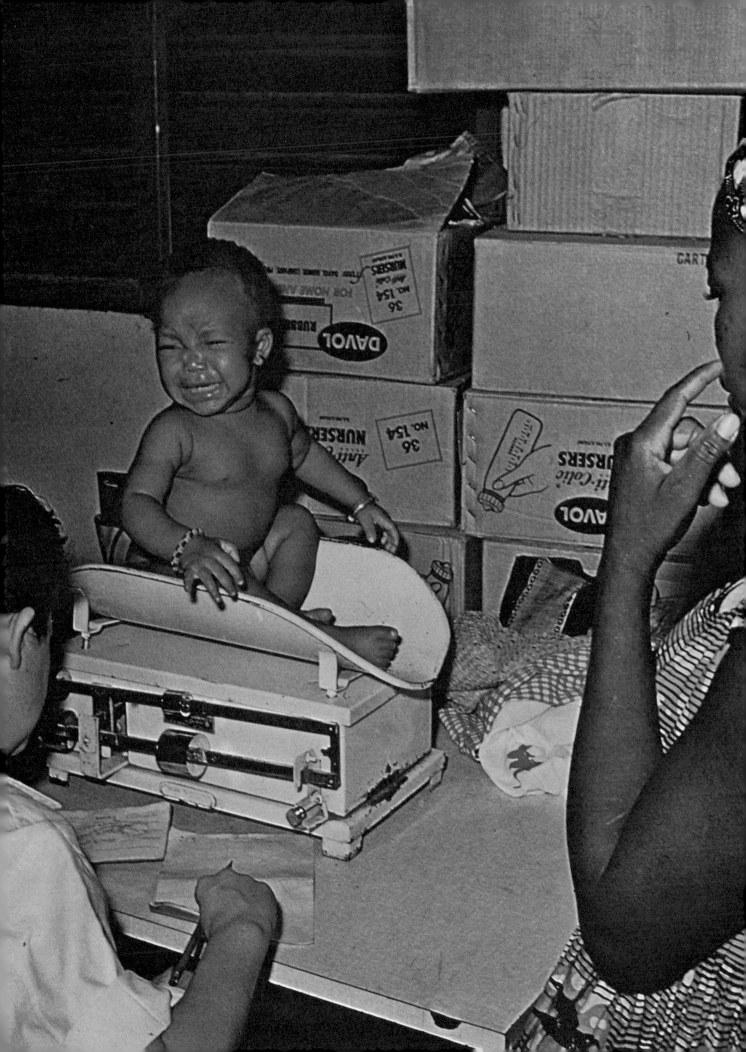

THE OBA: VANISHING DESPOT

THIS man has just about had this day. Granted, he and all he represents will always be remembered as part of Nigeria's colorful past, but the hope is that no one again will possess so much power or be so much the arbiter of life and death. He is a Yoruba *oba*—a special chief—dressed here in the ceremonial robes reserved for feasts of the god of iron. He carries a flywhisk as a symbol of his high rank. There was a time when people threw themselves to the ground in obeisance when the *oba* passed by, but that time is gone. The country's independence has curtailed his. He is still respected, but he is no longer feared because power is no longer in his hands.

Throughout Nigeria, the era of the despot is on the wane. The people know now that leaders should be servants of the public, not dictators. But suspicions linger, and there is fear of a strong central authority. Thus the three regions which formed the Nigerian federation insisted on their own autonomy, functioning as a unit only to a limited degree. Perhaps time will remove the lingering suspicions. Perhaps working together, even in loose federation, will convince the various regions that they can work together better as brothers than as neighbors. Only then will Nigeria be fully qualified to speak for freedom in Africa and in the world in a unified, resounding voice.

Nigeria has 8000 Girl Guides, and when they salute they promise to do their duty to God and Queen.

57

HOLIDAY IN GHANA: INDEPENDENCE DAY

WE HAVE traveled west now, one hundred and twenty-five miles across Dahomey (*duh-*ʜᴏʜ*-mee*) and Togo (ᴛᴏʜ-*go*), two former French territories now independent, and into Ghana, the second country on our tour. It appears we have arrived at a good time. This is Independence Day, March 6, and the country is celebrating.

As in similar celebrations elsewhere, this is a time for speeches, and the politicians are delighted to make them. Standing under the umbrella that is a sign of his importance is a young chief who is also a member of the Ghana Parliament. While performing his official duties in the capital city of Accra (*uh-*ᴋʀᴀʜ), he wears an ordinary business suit, but now it is Independence Day, so he is garbed in his traditional robes and decorations. This is, after all, the festival of nationalism and the young man knows what he is doing.

He is about to speak, and like all chiefs and politicians he will undoubtedly speak a long time. His speech will be longer today because he will not deliver it alone. Standing next to him is an aide called a linguist. The chief will address the linguist in a soft voice, then the aide will repeat the chief's words loudly for all to hear. If, by chance, the chief makes an undignified slip of the tongue, the linguist will not repeat these words but will say what was intended smoothly and correctly. Thus the young politician is protected from putting his foot in his mouth, a safeguard that perhaps should be more universally practiced.

As in Nigeria, many young, progressive chiefs have been elected to public office. Here, too, there is resistance among old chiefs to a strong federal government because of the loss of personal power it would entail. It is thus up to the young chiefs, many of whom have been educated abroad, to show that in a free country the power of the nation is in the hands of the people.

ACCRA: BACK-STREET STORE

THIS is an Accra street that few visitors get to see. It is around the corner from the enormous Makola (MAH-*koh-lah*) market, the busy shopping center of the city. What we see here, however, is a nameless alley that is known only to shoppers who are looking for bargains. This is the place of the day-old bread, the damaged merchandise, the surplus perishables and anything else the Makola merchants were left with that nobody wanted to buy. This is the place, too, for inexpensive trinkets or household items that must be sold too cheaply to interest the larger shopkeepers. It is not unlikely that here you will find a few things of value that disappeared from a Makola stall, while some irritated merchant in the market place is wondering what happened to them.

Notice the contrast between this street of tin roofs and the modern office building in the background. You will encounter this contrast frequently in Accra where, as in Lagos, a construction boom accompanied independence. The two cities also have this in common: they are both hot and humid. The newer buildings are air-conditioned, but outdoors, visitors wilt in a few moments and can only envy the Accra boys who run around in their khaki shorts.

Actually, Accra is a beautiful city. Its suburban homes are modern and spacious. The plush government office buildings, a few minutes from downtown Accra, have the cool, quiet efficiency of an up-to-date corporation. The city has pleasant parks with magnificent beaches nearby, and the Africa you came to see is only a short flight away.

CHIEF
BUTCHER
OF WA:
LEADING CITIZEN

PROUDLY wearing his Moslem robes, the chief butcher of Wa (WAH), in the Northern Territories, stands in front of his home at the end of a busy day. He is an important man in town. It is his duty to slaughter the cattle that will be sold in the market, and since most people in this area are Moslems, the process must be carried out according to orthodox regulations. The government requires that the butcher also make sure that the cattle are in good health before he slaughters them.

In this part of Ghana chief butchers inherit their positions, which adds to their eminence. Like chiefs, they have their own bands of musicians who, all their lives, never play for anybody else. The musicians go to the market in the morning, and as soon as the meat arrives they begin to play. Their music continues as long as the supply of meat lasts, and in this way everybody in town knows when the butcher shop is open and when the supply of meat has been sold. In the evening the musicians go to the butcher's house to serenade him, singing songs of praise — symphonies to steaks.

Giant anthills like this may have inspired the turreted buildings of northern Ghana.

The butcher's house is typical of those belonging to prominent Moslems. Strangely enough, the design is very similar to the towering anthills found in this part of the country. And the architects who built the United States Embassy in Accra evidently went to the ants for inspiration, too, and used a modification of this unusual style.

MODERN HOSPITAL: LEGACY OF BRITAIN

THIS hospital at Kumasi (*koo-*MAH-*see*), the capital of the Ashanti Region, is the finest in West Africa. Built by the British in 1956 at a cost of over eight million dollars, it also contains a nurses' training center. But Africans are always wary of anything new, anything they have never seen before, and the ultramodern hospital fell into that category.

At first, nobody would go into the building. When patients finally consented to enter, they insisted on remaining on the first floor so they could hop out a window easily in case they sensed any danger. To be put into an elevator and be swept up to the heights would be foolhardy, for who could hope to jump to safety then? In time, however, the people got used to the idea, then went to the opposite extreme. They discovered the splendid view from the upper floors and invited entire villages up to enjoy it.

A unique problem arose during the construction of the hospital. Precious to the Ashanti is a Golden Stool which, according to legend, was given to them by God and sent down from heaven on a black cloud. A tree was planted where it touched the ground; the tree still stands. The place is sacred and awesome to the Ashanti. When the hospital was designed, nobody realized that one wing of it came within feet of the tree. Not only was this sacrilegious, but surely no Ashanti would ever enter that part of the hospital, so the building had to be redesigned.

Few people have ever seen the Golden Stool; it is supposed to be the private possession of the Ashanti king. But thousands have seen the hospital as patients and witnessed the miracles of the white man—modern medicine. And from the hospital have gone scores of trained medical technicians to perform their own miracles. Many people rather suspect it is all possible because the hospital is so near the sacred tree.

HEALTH
LESSON:
TEACHING
WITH PUPPETS

IN TAKING its health program to the people, the Ghana government has found that the best way to teach is to entertain. This technique is especially effective in areas where illiteracy is high. Thus a traveling puppet show presents dramas to illustrate basic facts of hygiene. The audience laughs, joins in song with the puppets, and lessons in good health are taught painlessly and effectively.

Other precautions are taken. Bush people are traditionally wary of strangers—a painful lesson taught them centuries ago by the slave traders. For this reason, life-size photographs of the doctors and nurses who will soon be calling are put on display in the villages so that the people can get used to the sight of them. Then when the strangers arrive to do their work they need waste no time breaking down barriers, and villagers have the feeling, "Where have I seen you before?"

Today, all of Ghana is divided into medical districts, each with its own medical officer. Usually he is more of a trained nurse, qualified to make simple diagnoses and to give vaccinations, injections and pills.

A motorcycle clinic brings health and hope to patients in a remote village.

Severe cases are sent to the nearest hospital. The medical officer and his assistant travel on motorcycles, setting up their clinic under a tree in each village as they make their rounds. By hard work, skill and a few tricks, Ghana is slowly overcoming its health problems.

ROYAL
ORCHESTRA:
NOISY
BUT GOOD

THIS is the orchestra of the King of the Dagomba tribe, on its way to liven up one of his weekly audiences. The men are playing a single-stringed instrument called a *goji* (*go-jee*), similar to the *oud* (*ood*) of the Arabs and doubtless brought to this part of the world along with the Moslem religion. The other musicians are children shaking calabashes.

The orchestra plays as it approaches the palace, letting people know that the King is ready to receive them. The music is loud, it has a hefty beat, and if the King is known to be in a good mood the people fall in behind the band and dance their way to the palace. If, on the other hand, the King is known to be angry today, the public audience will be a short one. In either case, those who address him will do so properly, beginning always with the salutation, "Lion, lion, king, king, upholder of the universe," before coming to the point.

Unlike the Ashanti chiefs whose thrones are patterned after the Golden Stool, the great Ya-na of the Dagombas sits on a throne of lion skins and cushions. Courtiers and visitors sit on the floor with their backs to him because it is considered a mark of respect not to look directly at the Ya-na. During the audience, whenever the King utters a sound—a word, a cough, a sneeze—the courtiers snap their fingers and the orchestra breaks out in a few bars of ceremonial response. On days when the King has a cold or feels particularly talkative, the palace is a noisy place indeed. But these days, what with a Parliament at Accra making all the decisions, there isn't much for a King to do, so the weekly audience is mostly an occasion for fun—which everybody has.

THE CHIEF'S SHADOW: A LIFETIME JOB

THE solemn expression on this young man's face is understandable when you discover the position he holds in his Ashanti village. He is an *okra* (OH-*krah*) —the chief's shadow, and it is a position he will hold as long as he lives— or as long as the chief lives. The *okra* is not a bodyguard, not a servant, not even a companion. He just hangs around. He must never leave the chief's side, day or night.

Although the *okra*'s job assures him a comfortable life, it has one serious drawback. When the chief dies, his shadow must die too, whether he wants to or not. Clearly, then, when the chief is sick his *okra* has his own reasons for not feeling too well. *Okras* are appointed; they cannot refuse the appointment nor can they ever resign. Occasionally an *okra* happens to die first, which upsets the chief because it is a bad omen and that is why the position usually goes to a young man. The tradition of *okras* is fading in most Ashanti villages, but where it is retained there is invariably an exodus of young men whenever the job is available.

The brilliant patterns of African fabrics are marvelously varied and imaginative.

An *okra*'s costume is similar to a chief's—a toga made of *kente* (*ken-teh*) cloth. Brightly colored with beautifully intricate designs, *kente* cloth is made by hand, and a robe, which often takes weeks to complete, costs as much as a hundred dollars. An *okra* gets his free, but considering the risks of his job this is a minor fringe benefit.

70

ACCRA HARBOR: SPECIAL DELIVERY

ON THE seacoast, fishermen of the Fanti (FAHN-*tee*) tribe have an unusual specialty. Because the Accra harbor is so shallow, big vessels cannot draw near shore and must anchor a mile out. The Fanti paddle their famous Accra surfboats, which they have made by hand, and run a tender-service. Like tugboat operators, these boatmen get paid only when they work, so there is always fierce competition to meet an incoming ship far out at sea and escort her to her anchorage. There, cargo and passengers are taken aboard the surfboats.

The work is done with a great deal of shouting, screaming and laughter, and there is always singing to provide a rhythm for the rowers. In the surf near the shore, unloaders wait to carry the cargo to the beach, usually on their heads. If there are any passengers, they are expected to step from the bobbing boats into sedan chairs (called "mammy chairs") carried on the shoulders of husky stevedores. It is not unusual for cargo or passengers to get a dunking before reaching the beach.

While this is a picturesque way of doing things, it is not very efficient, and the days of the colorful Accra surfboats are numbered. At Tema (*teh*-MAH), once a romantic little fishing village seventeen miles up the coast, a splendid modern harbor has been constructed. The villagers were resettled nearby, and the new town was designed and built from scratch, embodying all the advantages of a planned community with well-balanced industries. Ships will dock here within the sheltering arms of breakwaters at fully equipped concrete quays. But it won't be the same. Progress sometimes takes the fun out of life.

BUS TRAVEL:
TOWN AND
COUNTRY

FOR years, the most popular mode of transportation in Ghana was the bicycle. But something new has been added in the cities: the municipal bus systems. To be sure, they are a welcome convenience, especially for women in their long Mother Hubbards, barefoot and burdened, who would otherwise have to walk. The luggage carried by the women shown here is not at all unusual on the average crosstown bus. It is a safe bet that already aboard is somebody with a couple of goats in tow. If you want to travel in Africa, you must endure African ways.

One of the most entertaining modes of African travel in the bush is the mammy wagon, an overcrowded open-air bus that you board the best way you can. Mammy wagons have routes and schedules but ignore both. Privately owned and often driven by women, mammy wagons are for travelers who don't care where they're going or when they get there. Traditionally, mammy wagons have slogans painted on their sunguards in English, the national language, though the humor is African.

The mammy wagon is a popular conveyance for passengers who travel light-heartedly.

"Though I have no fruits, Yet I cast Shadow." Others announce: "Love Is Nice" or "Man Is Weak" or "Wise Men Seldom Speak." At Tamale (*tuh-*MAH-*lee*) in the Northern Territories, is a bus bearing the profound advice: "Don't Beat Your Wife—Beat Her Mother."

FETISH
SHRINE:
POWERFUL
MAGIC

AT BURUFU (*broh*-FOO) up in the Northern Territories we see one of Ghana's principal fetish centers. Here witch doctors are still very important people. This shrine is for the Lobi-Dagarti (LOW-*bee-duh*-GAR-*tee*) tribe, who built it many years ago, but its popularity is such that people often come all the way from Accra to make their sacrifices here.

According to pagan belief, these statues are inhabited by spirits that can remove curses or impose them. A woman may sacrifice a chicken in hopes that the spirits will allow her to have a baby. A man about to go on a hunting trip will promise to sacrifice part of his catch if the spirits will bless his bow and arrow. Or a troubled man from Accra will offer up a goat with pleas that the curse put on him by an enemy be removed.

As odd as such things may sound to us, they are serious matters to the Ghana pagans, who comprise a majority of the population. Of particular significance is the power of the witch doctors indicated by these beliefs, a power that has long held Africa in its special darkness. Although it is a man's prerogative to worship as he pleases, the fear of curses and evil spirits that plays so large a part in African paganism has kept the continent enslaved as brutally as any outside force.

Thus it is certainly a good thing that missionaries are gradually eliminating paganism, replacing it with hope and love and trust and confidence in a benevolent God. And it is good, too, that the sheer force of civilization has penetrated the African jungle, putting knowledge where there was fear, tools where there was helplessness, dignity where there was the abjectness of the mentally enslaved.

THE NOBLE
GOAL:
POLITICAL
RALLY

IT IS ELECTION time, and once again the campaigners take to the bush trails with glowing tales about the wonderful candidates who deserve the people's vote. The best way to attract a crowd is to send out the news on a talking drum. The enormous instrument was used to transmit messages over great distances in Ghana long before the world dreamed of radios and telegrams, and today the Ghana Broadcasting System opens its news reports with a talking drum.

The people hear the drum, and from it they can tell what time the speeches will begin. They arrive; they listen; they decide. In a marvelous new way the people are as powerful as the old fetish spirits, for they can affect the future of a man, the future of a country; they have the vote. How they use their vote in these first years of self-government will determine how successfully Ghana achieves its goals.

Near Accra is Christiansborg Castle, built by Danish slave traders three hundred years ago and used now as the presidential mansion. Close by is a gleaming white structure, erected in 1957 when Ghana achieved self-government. It is called the Arch of Independence and upon it are the words: FREEDOM AND JUSTICE. These are now the birthright of all Ghanaians, the heritage for generations to come.

The Arch of Independence stands like a gateway to the new Africa whose people rule themselves.

SOME FAMOUS NAMES IN WEST AFRICAN HISTORY

HENRY THE NAVIGATOR (1394-1460)—*Prince of Portugal, who inspired and directed voyages of exploration down coast of Africa, resulting in Portuguese settlements in the area.*

CHRISTOPHER COLUMBUS (1451-1506)—*Genoese explorer, who is believed to have been a member of Portugal's expedition to Ghana, 1481-2.*

VASCO DA GAMA (1469?-1524)—*Portuguese navigator, leader of first successful voyage around Africa to the East.*

OSEI TUTU (d. 1731?)—*King of the Ashanti; great warrior and conqueror of many tribes.*

USMAN DAN FODIO (1754-1817)—*Fulani sheik, who in 1802 launched a religious war against pagans and created a Fulani empire.*

MUNGO PARK (1771-1806)—*Scottish explorer of Africa, who traced the upper Niger River course in 1796. On second Niger expedition he lost his life.*

HUGH CLAPPERTON (1788-1827)—*Scottish explorer of northern Nigeria.*

RICHARD LANDER (1804-1834)—*English companion of Clapperton. He continued explorations after his friend's death, and with brother John (1807-1839) discovered the Niger delta in 1830.*

SAMUEL AJAYI CROWTHER (1809-1892)—*Yoruba missionary of the Church of England, consecrated as first bishop of the Niger Territories in 1864.*

HEINRICH BARTH (1821-1865)—*German adventurer who traveled through the emirates of northern Nigeria in 1850-5, as only surviving member of his expedition, and later wrote fascinating account of trip.*

HERBERT MACAULAY (1864-1946)—*One of the leaders of Nigeria's drive toward independence, known as the "Father of Nigerian nationalism."*

DR. J. E. K. WEGYIR AGGREY (1875-1927)—*Noted Ghanaian educator, instrumental in the development of secondary schools in his country.*

SIR EMMANUEL QUIST (1882-1959)—*Distinguished Ghanaian lawyer and judge, first speaker of the National Assembly after independence.*

KWAME NKRUMAH (1909-   )—*First president of Ghana and leader of the Convention People's Party.*

ALHAJI ABUBAKAR TAFAWA BALEWA (1912-   )—*First prime minister of the Federation of Nigeria.*

AMOS TUTUOLA (1921-   )—*Nigeria's best-known author, who wrote* The Palm Wine Drunkard *and other stories and folk tales.*

SOME IMPORTANT DATES IN WEST AFRICAN HISTORY

c. 2000 B.C.	*Earliest iron-working culture of West Africa, the Nok, flourishes in central Nigeria.*
c. 600 B.C.	*According to Herodotus, Phoenician navigators make a three-year voyage around Africa on the orders of King Necho of Egypt.*
c. 1000 A.D.	*The city of Kano is founded in northern Nigeria.*
1076	*The great empire of Ghana in the Sudan is destroyed by Berber invaders. Its dispossessed inhabitants are thought to be the forebears of present-day Ghanaians.*
c. 1100	*Hausa tribes reach northern Nigeria, followed by Fulani invaders in the next century. Both bring Moslem influence to the area.*
1482	*Portuguese construct the first fortified trading post, Fort Elmina, on Ghana coast.*
1483	*Trade relations are established by Portuguese with Nigerian city-state of Benin.*
16th-18th centuries	*Throughout this period, Portuguese, English, Dutch, Danes, Swedes and Prussians compete for trading rights. Gold trade gives way to slave traffic, decimating native population.*
1807	*Britain declares slave trade illegal, as do other nations, but smuggling of slaves continues.*
1861	*Nigerian port of Lagos is annexed by Britain.*
1886	*Coastal Ghana becomes British crown colony of the Gold Coast. Ashanti territories are annexed in 1900.*
1903	*British troops gain control of northern Nigeria. In 1914 Nigeria becomes a single administrative unit under a governor-general.*
1957	*On March 6, the Gold Coast becomes independent Ghana, first Negro member of the British Commonwealth. On July 1, 1960, Ghana is proclaimed a republic.*
1960	*Nigeria gains its independence on October 1, and joins the Commonwealth.*

SOME WORDS AND PHRASES FOR NIGERIA AND GHANA

Although the official language of both countries is English, there are hundreds of tribal languages as well, with Hausa widely spoken in Nigeria and Twi in Ghana. Here is a list of words translated into those two native languages. The words are written in simple phonetics with the accented syllable in capitals.

ENGLISH	HAUSA	TWI
Good morning.	ee-NAH k'WAH-nah	neh-MAH woh ah-CHEH
Good-bye.	sigh WAH-tah RAH-nah	dah YEE-eh
Please.	in kah YEHR-dah	meh s'REH woh
Thank you.	nah GOH-deh	meh-DAH woh ah-SEH
Come in.	sheeh-GOH	brah dahng moo
Yes. No.	ee AH-ah	you da-BEE
Where is . . . ?	ee-NAH	eh-WOH hen
Today	yoh	ehn-NEH
Tonight	dah YEM-mah	ehn-NEH ah-nah-DOO fah
Tomorrow	goh-beh	oh-chee-NAH
Yesterday	JEE-ah	n'NEH-rah
How long . . . ?	YAH-yah sah-WON	ah-CHEH
How much . . . ?	NOW-ah	ah-HEN
Water	ROO-ah	ah-SOO
Food	ah-BIN-chee	ah-dwah-NEH
Man	moh-TOON	mah-REE-mah
Woman	mah-CHEH	ph-b'YAH
Child	YAH-roh	ah-koh-DAH-ah
Friend	ah-boh-KEE	n'yohn-KOH
Good	dah-KEH-oh	yeh
Bad	bah-KEH-oh	moo-OH
Boat	kwah-LEH-kwah-LEH	hem-BAH

NUMBERS

One	day-YAH	b'YAH-koh
Two	bee-YOU	ah-b'YEHN
Three	oo-koo	ah-b'yeh-SAH
Four	hoo-DOO	ah-NAHNG
Five	bee-YEHR	ah-NOOM
Six	shee-DAH	ah-s'YAH
Seven	bah-KWAY	ah-SOHNG
Eight	tahk-WAHS	ah-woh-TWEE
Nine	tah-RAH	ah-KROHN
Ten	GOH-mah	ee-DOO
One Hundred	dah-REE	oh-HAH
One Thousand	doo-BOO	ah-PEM

MONEY

Nigeria: Pound
        Shillings—twenty to a pound

Ghana: Pound
        Shillings—twenty to a pound

INDEX